TRUTH DE-CODE-IT

PORGANS

outskirtspress
DENVER, COLORADO

Contents

PROLOGUE

Truth De-Code-It is a living-testament of an eye-witness' account discerning Truth in an era of transparent deception espoused by billionaires, media moguls, government officials, and banking interests as they foster their orchestrated crisis-management cabal, showcased on Wall Street and around the world.

Their actions have given rise to an epiphany in-the-making, as we the people awaken to the irreconcilable Truth and deal with it accordingly; empowering us with the ability to change ourselves and the world.

The content of this book reflects upon the plutocracy's use of the revised-edition of the outdated Machiavellian script, to exploit, manipulate, and amass fortunes from public sources; as the moneychangers- and shepherds-of-deception fleece the unsuspecting flock.

This publication provides the means to partake in a natural-sustainable lifestyle, minimizing and eliminating life's uncertainties, while emphasizing and promoting mutual-Coexistence and self-empowerment as individuals-globally.

The message is simple, use discretion when patronizing banks and multinational conglomerates, buy less, lighten your footprint, live truthfully and strive to adopt a way-of-life that is economically and ecologically sustainable.

Truth De-Code-It transcends concepts of beginnings or ends, and realigns and reinforces our bond among ourselves and nature; wherein, Natural Law reigns. It views Life beyond human-induced limitations and sees it through an open-minded-spirited lens that recognizes all life as sacred.

It alludes to the "hocus-focus reel-time end-of-the world-crisis management scenarios" orchestrated, in part, by the profiteering-money changers' half-truths "erred" by mainstream-media airheads. If what you have read thus far is of interest, you are invited to peruse the contents and Epilogue: Truth-De-Code-It's Empowerment.

Dedication: This life's work in-the-making, a few mere utterances of Truth, are dedicated to my two best friends, Susan, my soul-companion, best friend and loving wife, and in everlasting-memory of my mother-in-law, Barbara, known to us as "Kid". I am eternally grateful to the Creator for making them a part of my life. GOD has bestowed upon me countless blessings, Susan is my most treasured.

APOTHEOSIS

Humanifestation-embodiment of the celestial dust

Rising up upon this earthen crust

Light - energy - motion

Divinely still - omnipotent

Taking form - transforming substance

Quintessential metamorphoses

Celestial body – mindful-soul

Simultaneously emerging-diverging-converging

Upon and within a perpetual interstellar multidimensional journey

Beginning - ending - forever transcending

Transiently encapsulated within this molecular frame

Serving as a medium to connect the indivisible and

Divisible incarnation of immortality

Revealing understanding which pontificates

The illusive abyss of incomprehensibility

Within and beyond the realm of human-deduced reality

Where earth and dust rise up -

Intangible form transforms substance

A cosmic continuum - a Transfiguration

APOTHEOSIS

HOMEOSTASIS AT THE OASIS OF GRACES

The Oasis of Graces resides within desolate places

For those in need of Homeostasis

Seek and ye shall find divinity in mind, body, and spirit

In the stillness of serenity

As a believer I am convinced Truth is Truth – deceit-less

By Grace, steadfast in my beliefs - I shall not be deceived

Soulfully knowing from all fears there is reverent relief

I walk in the light of the shadows of death

Spirited by the Nephesh - Life's breathe

I've awakened to the Risen Son - in a land

Where the sun never sets

Eternally and gratefully blessed not to hunger nor thirst

Immersed in the refuge at the Oasis of Graces

Giving eternal thanks and praises to my Creator

Yadah, Yadah, Yadah – Yeshua-Risen

OASIS OF GRACES

Harmonic Convergence

Eternal rays of Light neither Diminish nor Fade

They Simply Moves Across the Abyss in Waves

As the celestial Light Traverses Darkness of Space

It Illuminates Our Terrestrial presence on Earth

Pre-scripted Roles Imposed on Us since Our Conception

Foster Upon a Belief System Inundated with

Preconceived Misconceptions,

Half Truths and Outright Deception,

Flashbacks, Rejection,

Absent in the Presence of Self-Acceptance

The Essence of My Body, Mind and Soul are no Longer

Subjected to this Supposition

Empirically, I have transcended the bounds of this imposition

One must put ones' false beliefs to death

In order to experience the Oneness of life

Those who see all things as-One

Shall inherit the knowledge of Universal Truth

Captive minds shall be set free

Only when they speak truth with humility

Quantifying the unquantifiable is an exercise in futility

Timelessness -- Is Now -- a State of Mind

Clarity of Mind, absent of all Time

Dimensions of preconceived misconceptions cease to be

As Eternal Rays of Light Reflect My presence of being

Traversing within and beyond the boundaries of the

Known, and unknown Universes

As sunlight blends upon moonlit waters

I sense my Presence -- Enlightenment --

Harmonic Convergence within the Divinely-Created natural order

HARMONIC CONVERGENCE

TRUTHFULLY

Masses put to sleep by Media-induced apathy

Nations warring --- age-old conflicts soaring

Profiteer's reaping - Lame to be Leaping

Hide-a-ways --- seeking

Strong --- weakened

Market bottoming out --- peaking

Secured --- freaking

What are you thinking?

Titanic --- sinking

Word from Lincoln

Straight lines - right angles

Keep it simple – untangled

Thinking out of the box

Off the clock

Away from henhouse-foxes

Countrywide helps you out of your home

Unless, of course, you are a "friend" of Angelo's

Whispers of discontentment, heard hereabouts

"Living" in the absence of Truth

Undoubtedly, is dwelling in a house of ill-repute

Keep the window of your soul wide-open

Whilst you revere the awesome wonders of

Life's glorious splendor

Here-now and forever after

Living in accordance with Nature's laws

Learning from all, and, applying it

Truthfully

Cosmic Alignment

A cosmic alignment – Spiritual Renaissance - Incarnate

Is in the midst

Nature is mounting a restorative wind "a quick-fix"

All life is dependent upon it

As living beings it is imperative to be mutually interactive

To respect and revere Nature

By nurturing our relationship

Simply recognizing that Planet Earth and Nature

Is our life-support system

It is axiomatic - Killing nature is suicidal

Our way-of-life is out of the realm of natural order

The powers that be - profit off of "crisis management"

World conflicts and orchestrated mayhem

Taking its toll on all life forms

While pitching and branding the cabal as the "norm"

As the forces that be set the stage for the Perfect Storm

Hand-picked leaders from the variety pack

Go in knowing the "political game is rigged",

Cards are marked, deck is stacked

Plutocracy is robbing U.S. and

"We the People" are being forced to pay them back

If the cost for killing each other is becoming

Economically prohibitive

Simply stated, if for no other reason, budget slashing

Indicates it is no longer justifiably affordable

An in the best interest of life itself

The "It's All about Me" dog-eat-dog concept

Couldn't fly, float or swim

Or "History"

XY's Dogma, philosophies, monarchies, dictators

Emperors,presidents, CEO's, NGO's

And heaven knows, it isn't working!

The Greco-Roman philosophy served many emperors well

Render onto Caesar for all that want to pay

To pave their way to hell

Heaven knows we tried it

It's a Cabal – Orchestrated and –suicidal

Our ancestors will attest to that fact

That "civilizations" rise and fall

To wit, there has been enough endless self-ingratiation

Under the auspices of rulers, borders, and nations

We are all one and the same beings

Every precious life is special

And all the Earth-around is Sacred

Even before "X–XY"

ONE-existed in spiritual form and tangible substance

In good conscience I live

With, and for the common good

Along the way

Learning to discern and comprehend

All things in my presence

Being and experiencing life

Within this microcosmic-terrestrial shroud

Gazing into the star-lit night

Eyes closed sensing the deafening sounds of silence

Peace, refuge, tranquility

Made way into the hearts of all humanity

Conditions that exists, became that way,

And can be fixed accordingly

As a Solutionist

One witnesses much

As does many

Life is an adventurous journey

Albeit, Live It

With open hearts and unclenching fists

Remembering, we are all in this together –

And approach it, accordingly

The world as we have come to know it

Is undergoing phenomenal natural and human-induced changes

Adaptation and disassociation

In participating in the exploitation of life - essential

In cases to simply increase corporate profits

Which are already rife with all-out corruption

Subject to endless supposition

In a "way-of-life" that inspired delusion

Answers to questions are front-end loaded

When they don't work there's an implosion

Setting in motion the "crises-management modus operandi"

Prompting trillions of dollars in government give away programs

To the Goldman banksters' hell-bent

At buying up and selling the planet we live on

Apparently, clueless, of the consequences

Associated with their actions

Although, quite "profitable" and seemingly didactic

Others see it as irreprehensible, vulgar,

Bordering on the fringe of insanity

And as the aftermath of an atrocity in the making

Its' always been that way! Yes. Indeed, for many

But should not be for any one forever more

With my feet planted on terra firma

I gaze from within and upon the Cosmic Realm

Of bewilderment, as by Grace,

I remain-in-alignment –

Oblivious to any way but what it is terrestrially,

Elementally and, of course,

Cosmically-Aligned

REIGNING AWAY

It's a New-Heavenly Day on Earth

No longer to conquer or dominate

Rather to live in mutual coexistence - Naturally -

The masses need to walk away from Wall Street's

Billionaire-dead beats

Taking people out of their homes

Putting families on the street

Espousing the need for Homeland Security

Which, begins by having a home

The same group is yelling "support the troupes"

To protect their investments abroad

Raising the question as to how low can they go?

Can "We the People" afford to eat the billionaires' debt?

While they amass fortunes off of the backs of the masses

And turn around and have us paid them for doing it

This blatant disregard raises contempt

There is an apparent need for the masses to write its own script

All my love to each and everyone

In this wondrous journey

Living, learning, sharing and giving thanks

By sharing and applying the knowledge, wisdom and all the

Gifts presently

Living our life's accordingly – as a new-dawn is reigning upon us

Reigning Away

Truth Decay

Is an oxymoron

However, moronic behavior appears to be the prevailing paradigm

Speaking Truth is paramount to committing a crime

In the interlude of this enigma

Truth has become stranger than fiction

As we denied the obvious and placate what we cannot obfuscate

Our world, lives and mortal fate

Are hinged on half-truths, orchestrated deception and outright denial

Gambling with Life - going for broke

As Earth's jungles go up in smoke

Mutual assured destruction - to keep the peace

Suicidal lifestyles - fixed and inflexible

Single-minded process - absent of reality

Living plants diagnosed with terminal cancer

The host is being put to death

While others are killing to avenge the dead

White man's dream is colored blind

Race victimization - a global expectation

Tribal realities and tribulations

Spear-headed by Presidential dictations

Truth has been compromised

It is acceptable to lie

So-called leaders being lead

Portraying a dream that has long-been dead

Lives filled with emptiness

Homeless being dispossessed

Televangelist byting for the almighty dollar

Bush whackers ripped-off Silverado

Goldman's Wall-Street Heist Trump's Bernie Madoff

Holy wars mixing' blood and oil

Entrepreneurs profiting from turmoil

Iron curtail was just a shield

New world order another bad deal

It makes it easier to control and steal

Self-denial and unforeseen realization

Self-indulged materialization

Concepts of reality - unreal

Rich feasting - hungry without a meal

Free enterprise system holding "U.S." hostage

Endless thoughts - timeless concepts

Memory programmed to forget

Prosperity incurred by debt

Freedom and Peace mercantile sublimations

Reinforced by dictatorial recantations

United States - a divided nation

Difficult to relate - let alone understand

Over our heads on dry land

Telecommunications probing deep into space

Out of touch here on Earth

Waiting on hold for tomorrow

For what humankind refuses to reconcile

A state of self-induced denial

Before our eyes these truths are disclosed

As the fundamental principles of our civilization decompose

TRUTH DECAY

PLUTOCRACY RULES! SAYS WHO? YOU!

Upper class – pushing the envelope

Crises syndrome – Portraying visions of hopelessness

Whilst billionaires profit from their daily fix of greediness

The masses are losing faith and walking away from Wall Street

Investments there are anything but safe

Plutocracy manipulating and exploiting the "free-market" place

Apparently, if the "Price is Right" you can afford to live in disgrace

Just how safe it safe

When you can't bank on the Bank

Anti-semantic rhetoric is showing signs of major blowback

It's difficult to practice what one preaches

Learning is set by the example of the teacher

Palestinians-Human Rights-Dignity-Freedom

Is an unresolved holocaust

The absence of peace flies in the face of tolerance and

Mutual-coexistence

It's a hard row to hoe – on the path of least resistance

Notwithstanding, indifference is not a viable option

If what we have been misled to believe isn't the Truth

If all else fails always be true to yourself

Preaching the fear of the Creator from pulpit of Hell

Generates a foul smell of elevated levels of

Toxic-synthetic excrement

Justifying a one-time appointment with "Doctor Kevorkian"

Who in Hell do the billionaires think they are,

Don't they reside on this planet under the same star?

Even an Agnostic, a non believer,

Has to have a conscience – a heart

Blind-sighted by earthly treasures and fleshy pleasures

The discourse of their life's journey will be a testament to

Self-ingratiation

Leaving behind a tragic Legacy

Of unimaginable wealth and orchestrated disparity

Shadow-dancing in the artificial-light of ages of

Human-induced darkness

The so-called learned ones espouse outdated

Machiavellian Rhetoric

As a means to control and misdirect the masses

Who sacrifice their precious lives for worthless-expectations

Rife with self-indulgence and planned obsolesces

Nevertheless, it is what it is for those that choose it to be

Albeit, buying in and selling out is nothing short of

Economic-enslavement

Inconsistent with the inalienable rights

Endowed upon and within every human being

Masses linked to their iPods, blackberry, and lap tops

Seeking to be a part of the informational rage

Playing out their lives in cyber space

Attempting to keep pace on worldwide web superhighway

Co-dependent on an unreliable communication complex

With highly vulnerable traits

Band width, solar flares,

Sun cycles and magneto disturbances-history in-the-making

If, of course, I AM, not mistaken

Woe on to those with grandiose intentions

It can be contentious, i.e., half-baked thoughts from

Sir Francis Bacon

Dominion and conquering Nature a blatant oxymoron

Freud and Darwin missed the Mark and the Twain shall never meet

Ancestral roots climbing out of trees

Big Bang – raising reasonable doubts as to how

Creation got jump-started

Prime-mortal soup – more Hog wash

Parallel universes bordering on dementia

Sigmund - Mother, Mother, Mother – Oh! Please, stop

Doctorial candidates and scientists on the cusp of making

Something else up

Now, it is the "God-Particle" a force field

That permeates universal mass

As the masses slough it off as more academic-illogical hypothesis

Academic-brain "functioning" but no body's home

Extinction is being studied to death

Speaking the Truth is a major threat - So-be-it

Nevertheless, if one is seeking the Truth, begin within yourself

"We the People" should not be subjugated to plutocratic rules

United together the Machiavellian-Plutocracy cannot stand

"We the people" enabled the plutocrats to become sickly-rich

United-together we have the individual-collective empowerment

To redistribute the wealth,

Buy-taking steps not to patronize the multinationals

Plutocracy's Rules?

TRADE WINDS SHIFT

Dragon rising out of the East

Communist China capitalizing off of the Free-enterprise system

Entrepreneurs undermining the precepts of American beliefs

Spewing bits and bytes of everything but what it appears to be

As the garment of our beliefs are being torn at the seams

All that was held precious is being trumped by greed

We the people are living out a horrific fantasy

As all we held sacred appears to be vanishing

Crisis cabal orchestrated by the plutocracy

Freedom is being offer by Chase in the form of a credit card

Pushing from the left and pulling from the right

In the midst of a moving target just beyond our line of sight

Borrowing money to fund the spread of "demockcracy"

Placing U.S. deeper in the red

Debt and death plagues the West

As the rising dragon awakens in the East

The media-military-industrial complex continues to feast

As we fight wars under the guise of promoting peace

Homeland insecurity heightens

As more families are forced out of their homes onto the streets

Government has become buy-functional

As the plutocrats race to privatized publicly-owned resources

The tidal winds of "history" are shifting

As the simplicity of life has become exponentially more complicated

Heaven's knows we cannot conceal

Thoughts of injustice, indifference or

Disparity, within or amongst ourselves

Unless, of course, we have hell to pay

On this field of pain and sorrow

The Spirit of Life lifts its voice signing away for a better tomorrow

Knowing unconscionable thoughts will not rest upon hallow ground

As is in the deafening sound of absolute silence

We are over whelmed by endless violence

And, yet, and still, we rise up to be inspired

Guided by the enduring light and a passionate fire

Destruction of limb and life

In the nether world of sink or swim

The ideals of truth, compassion, and justice

Replaced by the Golden Idol of let's make a deal and compromise

Wherein it is befitting to be unreal

Where the price of living is equal to the wages of sin

And yet, they seek for all the more of what they can't get enough

To embed the seed of fear of the Creator

Into the heart of humanity is inhumane

A Diabolical oxymoron

Casting aspersion under the guise of Truth

Emanates from the core of evil

Negating the reality that all life forms are sacred

And yet, there is less to remember and even more to forget

If, what is now viewed as a way-of-life

As good as it gets

Then, there should be no reason but to put it to rest

The Ideals promoted by the one-percent

And blaze a new path toward peaceful coexistence

Mutually beneficial for the other 99-percent

On that note of eternal hope

Hence, I harkened to the cacophony of song birds

Bursting forth in the dawning light of divinity

As I stand and mutually coexist

I witness the light of day through the multifaceted lens

Of the dragonfly

Perched securely on the blade of a reed blowing in the wind

And in the not so far distance

I heard the sounds of a fading melody of a bygone generation

And still, I sense the living embodiment of all things

Immersed in the glorious omnipresence of nature's serenity

Residing and abiding in the realm of the Kingdom's domain

Unencumbered – unafraid

Celebrating this gift of life each and every day

Giving eternal thanks and praise to live a life so blessed by Grace

Truthfully, albeit, I see a dragon flying-rising out of the East

And the fate of the West is blowing in the Wind

As traitors buy, trade, and sellout the U.S.

May we rise to reconcile this conundrum

And shift the trade winds back so as to be mutually favorable

To once again become productive and sustainable

So that the spirit of the wind will renew

Each of us and future generations

As the Trade Winds shift

SHEPHERDS OF DECEPTION

Conceptual deception woven within the web of

Preconceived-fundamental misconceptions

Dogma, traditions, ideological concepts

Forster upon a "belief system" adopted by our ancestors

Delusive concepts - misguided beliefs

Many chained to primordial soup, parallel universes,

Shredded "strings"

And/or the yet-to-be found "missing link"

Albeit, "Experts" immersed in deck-chair debate

As the Titanic sinks

Big Bang theory shot full of holes

By the Galileo probe

As the so-called learned ones

Espouse their latest esoteric theories from cyber towers

Humanity misled by the shepherds of deception

Their "sole" intention is to fleece the unsuspecting flock

Shadow dancing in the artificial light of human-induced darkness

Drawing us farther away

From the essence of our "soulful" enlightenment

Humankind held powerless in pursuit of "absolute-power"

Having lost sight of the ALMIGHTY

Mindsets fixed on moving targets

Getting less - striving harder

Orchestrated mayhem in the "free-market"

Ruling class perpetuates division

While, sharing in the windfall profits

Self-induced madness at biblical proportion

Generations degenerating via inherent distortions

Human disorder conflicting with the Natural Order

This discord will be overcome accordingly

Humanity cast adrift in a way of life

Inundated with tormenting thoughts,

Conflicting messages, with deadly consequences

Contemporary living, the dichotomy of meaningless superficiality

Placated in a mass state of pseudo-comatose reality

Self-destructive fixation

Predicated, in part, on `Darwinian's" misconception

Of survival of the fittest

Therein lies an oxymoron that now threatens all species existence

A concept that preempts harmonic convergence

Via mutual co-existence (COEXISTANCE)

This death wish is a living testament

To those insidiously deceptive concepts

Absent of Godliness

SHEPHERDS OF DECEPTION

Celestial E=MC Square – Dancers

Eyes to see – Ears to hear

Magnanimous Creator's (MC's) cosmic gas

Celestial dancers kicking up stardust

Upon this earthen crust

Keenly attuned to the realization that there is no future nor past

Eternally stepping – sharing – in this omnipotent experience

As the effervescence of one's Spirit lifts

As the ebb and flow of the cosmic alignment shifts

We partake in this celestial dance

Knowing that in the Creator's understanding – we are understood

The simplistic common denominator

Is equal to all things of and by God are good

Hence, why sink or swim – when you can float

Take note of the tear in the turtle's eye

Hearken to why it cries

Heaven Knows - keep on floating

With faith there is absolutely nothing less than eternal hope

Trust in God's incomprehensible understanding and Divine Plan

Thus all things will be made known

Rising up boldly - overcoming fear

So far – to nowhere

She is the quintessential child shrouded in an ancient soul

Who keeps on floating – never growing old

She is the embodiment of the turtle's tears

Humbly asking what she has done to be a deserving one

A washed and immersed in the Eternal Sea of Celestial Souls

Heartfelt for the turtle's tears

God knows she is blessed

As a witness, I also attest for being blessed

To partake in this Celestial Dance

To live, love, and cherish this up lifting Spirit of mutual Coexistance

Faith gives rise to the quintessential effervesces

Enlightened Spirit spontaneously ubiquitously aromatic

For she has eyes to see and ears to hear

I know here now as I knew her then

An enlightened soul cannot buy into the white lie

Because it can't float and it doesn't fly

That's why a floater knows why a turtle cries

See eyes floating by

I know you and you know I

Flying through, in, and over the by-and-by

Tears are tears in the eyes of eyes

If the Spirit doesn't float or can't fly, it remains blind

Indifferent to the tear in the turtle's eye

Albeit, not your nor mine

As we dance and float in the celestial divine

Why then does the turtle cry?

God knows

Cosmically attuned to the Alpha rhythms

As we dance our way in and betwixt the gaps of our brain synapses

Contextually weaving in and beyond the vortex of the

All encompassing void

Amidst everything and nothingness

Being - Yet not being possessed -

In the presence of Divinity's interwoven Spiritual blissfulness

Blessed within and beyond mortal comprehension

Words of praise sensed – but unspoken

All the thanks I could give would only be a token

Confined by nothing but the wide-open cosmos

As we keep on ecstatically dancing and floating

Celestial - E=MC Square – Dancers

FIXING TIME – UNTIMELY FIXATION

Hands of time fixed by humankind

A notion that continues to elude the best of minds

Light years of darkness

Spent senselessly attempting to make sense

Out of theoretic senselessness

Passing by -- spinning still

Moving in place -- within an ecliptic sphere

Eternally spacing out in the universal now and here

Heavenly body -- cosmically aligned

Impassive to the hands of time

Dimensions expanding --- Universes contracting

Actively reacting

A matter over molecular dynamics

Quantum Physics -- cerebral physic

Fields of motion -- vacuum-packed motionless

Electrical chemical synapses -- thought provoking

Setting in place -- locomotion

Brain storming within the cortex an untimely reaction

Divinely and timelessly still -- A Universal constant

Does anyone really have a fix on whether time exist

I haven't a notion

Fixing Time - Untimely Fixation

PRE-SCRIPT SHUN – SHUNNING PRESCRIPTION

Spin doctors reeling out of control

Men of the cloth selling their souls

Underachievers in leadership roles

Psycho babblers - Babble-on

New beginnings beset by endless goodbyes

Subscribing to the same-old diatribe

Without ever asking why

Mixed messages - revolving doors

Never again B forever more

Preaching peace while waging wars from behind Temple walls

As the age-old battle rages on

Cyclical process - cycles on

Caught up - bogged down

Moving in place on the merry-go-round

Mindless meeting of the minds

A misnomer or simply symptomatic of a new beginning

Beyond the end times

Upper class dominated by low-lifers

Aspiring for the heavens- bogged down in the trenches

Sanctimoniously attempting to make sense out of dementia

Painstakingly digging up the past

As we lay the ground work to bury ourselves

So-called portrayers-traitors of truth

Promoting adulterated deception

Seeking truth under false pretenses

Blame-storming sessions orchestrated by the transgressors

Living life under a self-imposed death sentence

Denial a way of life

Acting indifferent to its irreconcilable consequences

Knowing, but saying it is not so, holding on to letting go

Common sense - senselessly uncommon

Long-term shortsightedness

Lives filled with emptiness

Misdemeanors - high crimes - played out via-prime time

Scales of justice weighted upon a shifting fiduciary paradigm

Facilitators and manipulators promoting the same old-script

Breed fear - Get rich quick

Selling out - Buying in - Shutting up - Giving in

Profiteers making out like bandits

Upper crust banking BIG TIME on downsizing

Outright class segregation predicated on economic enslavement

Striving to rise for the ultimate fall

Fortune -- misfortune befalls us all

Tranquilized by sublimely insidious trivia

Myopic visionaries lost sight of the big picture

Open minded to endless deception

Awaiting the coming of their leader the son of perdition

One nation under GOD in a state of abomination

Patients - Victims of Spin Doctors' prescriptions

Pre-Script Shun - Shunning Prescription

Cognitive Dissonance

Illusive signs - Decisive illusions

Substantive meaning - Meaningless substance

Effortless motion - Motionless

Outrage, disgust - Disgustingly outrageous

Liberated concepts - Sublimely confined

Generations degenerating - Inclined to decline

Misdirected directives - Illicit perceptions

Fundamental contradictions -

Prefaced on preconceived misconceptions

Unification neutralized - Monopolistic monarchies

Allegiance of recantation-United States a divided nation

Repetitive deception - Socially accepted

Freedom at any cost - A lost cause

Inalienable rights in suspended animation

Exercising freedom leads to incarceration

Open space confined by fences

Truth formulated by consensus

Barbaric civilization in a state of self-induced alienation

Cognitive Dissonance ©

TESTIVINTY

Courage, Wisdom, and Serenity

Through Him, With Him and In Him

I have been graced with Triple Indemnity

GOD, Son and Spirit - Holy Trinity

The worldly conflicts are beyond His refuge

I am consoled in the Eye of the storm

I am the ethereal composed in substance as I AM transformed

Yet, behold from whence I stand, I sense the stillness calmed

Embraced within HIS Loving arms

Death is in the hand of those that wield the sword

Winning and losing are both a lost cause

In HIM - I Am - Now and Forevermore

Aware of All Things - Bound by none

Serving in Accordance with HIS Will and Divine Law

I witness, see, and reflect on what I saw

No one can truly served more than just One-Almighty GOD

Now is a Constant

GOD's Enduring Love Is an Open Door

Winging It into the Here-Now and Forevermore

Earth is the Threshold to Heaven's Gate

We are Blind-sighted by Faith

Walk the Narrows

Keep it straight

Love is Love

Hate is Hate

Be-in now - Mean's now it's never too late

Open your Heart or seal your Fate

Without GOD there is no Escape

It's a one-way ticket to Heaven's Gate

Through Him - In Him- with Him

GOD–Son-Spirit=Trinity

Albeit, I Am, a living

Testivinty

ENIGMA TRANSFIGURED

Greatest Mysteries - Oldest Quest

Living Life - transfiguring Death

Understanding the Enigma without a Rosetta Stone

Accepting Intuitively the Truth we have always known

The Golden Rule is not a Riddle

It is just that Simple

Common Sense - Senselessly Uncommon

Indifference - A Now-a-Day Phenomenon

Discordantly Cut Away from the Accord

Living Life on the Edge of a Double-Bladed Sword

Balance of Power - A Shifting Paradigm

Sugar Coated Concepts - Decaying Our Minds

Mind over Matter - What Matters over Time

Is Time Matter Less

The Origin of Life, the Solar System, Universe for many

Still remain a heated debate

Were they Divinely-Created

Or a by-product of happenstance

Is Death the inevitable end to Life?

Or is it the exodus to Life Everlasting?

The Enigma for those that choose to Know

Is simply self-explanatory

It reside in the recesses of our Souls

Pontificating the abyss betwixt Life and Death

Arose at that instance when the Messiah

Crossed over the vertical and horizontal axis

Transfiguration, unveiled the Enigma –

As the common denominator

MY GOD - MY LORD - MY SAVIOR

Enigma Transfigured

Goldman's TEAM Sacking U.S.

We're in the throes of the ebb and flow of anything goes

Everybody see's it – nobody really seems to know

As we ultimately reap what we sow

So what! Everybody sees it – but many don't appear to know

Hanging by our finger nails – while standing on our toes

As it becomes increasingly more difficult to hold the

Culpable accountable

America-scams peaking out on the crescendo

Goldman TEAM (Take Everything Americans Make)

No mistake, it's the TEAM mentality

Everybody sees it, does anyone really want to know

Talking-heads airwave princes and princesses

Orchestrating the "reel show"

Mega-buck payoffs-bonuses to corporate-banking CEOs

Who have driven the national debt to an all time high

And the dollar to an all-time low

Hey! Everybody sees it – does anyone really want to know

Or wait, and get out of their-own way,

When there is no other way to go

Don't ask! Don't tell

Elizabeth Warren or the public where the

$700+ billion bailout went?

To whom, and for what

Funding Homeland Security

When there is no home to go – is outhouse insanity

Moving ever so fast and yet, ever so slow

Digging ourselves ever so deeper into a bottomless hole

Everybody sees it – does anyone really want to know

Hanging on by our fingernails while standing on our toes

Or, don't ask – don't tell

Contract with America set the stage for the

Wall Street bailout giveaway

TEAM Goldman manipulating the "free-market"

With a masterful stranglehold

The aftermath of the subprime banking foreclosure scam

Is adversely affecting more and more Americans

While the Nation's 50 state's Attorneys Generals, top cops

Sat around making a deal with the culprits

As the one-percentile's profits go beyond and outside the margins

The 99-percentile are being socioeconomically marginalized

Half-of-all-the developed world's wealth has vanished!

Did it really ever exist, other than on the worldwide web?

As the money changes cash in on all of this orchestrated mayhem

They leave us holding on to letting go

Knowing, but saying it can't be so

As the occupy demonstrators

Victims of the Goldman scheme - face retaliation

From the very government that has failed

To protect them from the banks

And, as it turns out, "We the people" are footing the bill

Goldman's Secretary of the Treasury Paulson

A primary orchestrator of the foreclosure cabal

And government coup d'etat

According to Congresswoman Kaptur interviewed by film producer

Michael Moore Capitalism: A Love Affair

All Hail! And, then, there was "To Big to Fail"

The testimony and documents say it all

The American Dream is being sold out by the Goldman TEAM

Free-Market is in a Free Fall

As the Almighty Dollar is being morphed

Into a new currency Chimerica

As the rising dragon awakes in the East

The Wall Street mongrel continue to feast

As the victims protest in the streets

Taking yet another beating to express their beliefs

Subject to harm, injury, and/or incarceration

The Result of the authorities failure to hold the thieving

Banksters accountable

Everybody see it – although, many are acting as if they didn't know

Goldman Sacking of U.S. EBB as Cash Flows

TIMELESS ZONE

Body, Mind, Soul-Unfold

The concept of time strikes a ring of death

Because it measures life in breaths

In the heart of my soul

My mind's-eye knows

The Spirit of my being dwells in a timeless zone

Minds constrained in the realm of human-induced limitations

Deprive themselves of the full realization

That they are the embodiment of the

Creative and Everlasting Spirit

The eternal light merely cast us

In the image of our present being

Yet, it does not set us apart from being

All-things eternally

TIMELESS ZONE

HOLY AXIS

Historical record based predominantly on half truths --

Legends and GOD only knows

Underachievers in overdrive

So-called purveyors of truth promoting the big lie

Brush fires raging out of control

Devil's advocates in leadership roles

The Prince of Darkness walks in the light of day

The Spurious Messiah is setting unenlightened souls on fire

The unquenchable thirst of greed is self consuming

The prospect of doom appears to be all enduring

Hell's angels are quoting Scripture from the Holy Bible

Temple dwellers making money like it's going out of style

The sons and daughters of the Pharisees and Scribes

Are holding court

Carrying out their traditional prosecution of the purveyors of truth

Justice prevails on a sliding scale -

Weighted in favor of the perpetrators

The so-called death of GOD via scientific consensus

Holds as much credence

As the yet-to-be-found missing link ideology

The essence and/or presence of absolute Truth

Will never be fully revealed

In a controlled study by an overly educated intellect's myopic mind

Attempting such an endeavor

Would be comparable to quantifying the unquantifiable

In a vacuum, which is simply the quintessential

State of Alienated denial

Divinity resides in the souls of all beings

Individually we are a reflective manifestation of the collective-

Spiritual conscientiousness

LORD Knows that the Paradigm of Everlasting Salvation abides,

Whereupon the horizontal and vertical axis Cross

HOLY AXIS

TAJ'S MIRAGE-ILLUSIVE FACADE

In pursuit of the illusionary facade - the Taj's Mirage

So easy to make it so hard

Keeping ourselves from being a-part from and with God

Getting in our own way every step of the day

Speaking ad nauseam without anything substantive to say

It's what you do - Not what you say

The Word in the Flesh has been sent

Take heed or make preparations for a cataclysmic event

All hell's breaking loose from Heaven's Gate

If you are bound to earth there is no escape

Keep to the narrows - Get it straight

Love is Love - Hate is Hate

Desert the Desert's burning fire of unquenchable thirst

Find refuge in the oasis of your eternal soul

If you can't sense the presence of Heaven

It's because you're bound on earth

Giving it all up for what it's worth

The illusionary pursuit of the Taj's Facade

So near - so far

So easy - to make it - so hard

When Loving You - is Loving GOD

Taj's Mirage-Illusive Façade

Concepts of Origin

Concepts of origin changing hands for a handful of change

Simply profound or profoundly strange

Prior to the reign of the pharaohs to the present hour

Humankind held powerless -- in pursuit of absolute power

While the so-called learned ones

Espouse unfounded theories from their ivory towers

Cling-on's holding fast

Transfixed in the future

Locked in the past

The rich and famous come first

Everyone else -- Last

Primitive cultures absorbed in the New Age

Ancestral knowledge lost in the informational craze

Super computers left to rage

Overload in cyberspace

Technological evolution in bits and bytes

Contained in a state of virtual reality

At a designated web site

Genetically engineered clones sitting on the throne

African Bushmen deposed from their ancestral homes

As De Beer's profits from the Diamonds forever mindset syndrome

Avon woman's in the Amazon

Ageless bodies - timeless minds

Nature remains indifferent to who lives or dies

As the Rate of death out paces life

Moving too fast, in place, to alter our fate

Preaching love - Reflecting hate

Policing the world to enforce peace

When it is unsafe to walk our city street

Progress paved by way of destruction

Minds control via seduction

Evil does not confine itself to color

It comes in all shades

Truth on the other hand is colorless

Bottoming out at the top

Image awards for being a first class flop

Isolated concepts of living devoid of life's true concepts

Living for tomorrow deprives us from living life fully today

Fortune, power and fame are a winning hand in a losing game

Nothing remains the same

Everything else is subject to change

In the course of human events

Dreams are lost and lives are spent

GOD given rights are heaven sent

The keys to the Kingdom are within our grasp

There is absolutely no fear

In the presence of Absolute Love

Simple concepts are understood

When the illusion of confusion are over come

Living here and now

Enables us to perceive the origin of our indivisible conception

Concepts of Origin

Burning Daylight 24-7

IN NEW-AGE OF ENLIGHTENED DARKNESS

Burning Daylight 24 - 7

Juxtaposed between Earth and Heaven

In the New-Age of Enlighten Darkness

Throwing out preconceived misconceptions

Unfounded theories - Supported by endless asinine rhetoric

Nothing, is without question an unquantifiable given

Everything else is subject to supposition

Being consumed in pursuit of the Ethereal

Time-maxed to the death null

Burning Daylight 24 - 7

Sucking-down micro-waved bytes of nuked delights

Fasting from the Manna from Heaven

Alienated from the Source of Creative - Spirituality

Living in the confines of a human-deduced reality

One-breathe away from transcending mortality

Instructed to cling on to whatever sticks

Hocus Focus - Reel-time - Bag of tricks

Scientific Breakthroughs - Latest Version of the So-called Truth

Tele-prompted authoritative figureheads - clueless

No one ever found any Universal Truth that did not always exist

They simply became aware - Enlightened to It

So-called Enlightened Souls - Are merely mortal Beings

Spiritually Attuned to the Divine Chi-quency

While others' are still statically impaired by their

Channeling and susceptibility to alienated Dogmatic Freak-quencies

Peace, Love, and Harmony are a Cosmic-resonating constant,

That remains within our grasp - Not beyond our reach as preached

They are a manifestation of our present state of being as

One - in All Things

Burning Daylight 24 - 7 - Searching for Shangri-la

While being juxtaposed between Earth and Heaven

One's relationship with the Divine

Is not contingent upon the wishes, whims or dictates of another

It is simply, and Truly GOD given

NEW-AGE OF ENLIGHTENED DARKNESS

BURNING DAYLIGHT 24-7

Human Being – Being Human

FEAR

Breeds, securely in the unknown

IGNORANCE

Is absence of knowledge

KNOWLEDGE

Is a thought known

LONELINESS

Is always present until you find yourself

Even so, without GOD, you may always be alone

SACRIFICE

Is in the giving

HAPPINESS

Is in the sharing

DESIRE

Is the need of having to be had

PEACE

Is a manifestation of our being in touch with our self and all things

IDENTITY

Is the element of self-acceptance

FREEDOM

Is an unconfined state-of-being

WAR

Is an action executed in the line-of-duty

DESTRUCTION

Is a manifestation of the destroyer's unawareness of beauty

DEATH

Enables us to transcend mortality

LIFE

Itself, is death defying

HOPE

Provides us with the will to survive

FAITH

Provides us with Eternal Life

TRUTH

Is a self-evident principle which cannot be

Realistically changed or distorted

Whether, it is, or is not understood, i.e., all things are One

LOVE

Absolute Truth, forgiveness, acceptance, understanding,

Fear understood

A Mainfestation of the Omniscient Being --

Who breathes the Breath-of-Life into all

Living things and Human Beings

HUMAN BEING --- BEING HUMAN

TEMPLE OF BLOOM

A View from a Room at the Temple of Bloom

Beneath the canopy of the celestial sky

Life in all her splendor is simply death-defying

The Temple of Bloom sits as a crowning jewel

Translucently illumining

As the eternal spark of the ethereal spirit breathes

Seeds of eternal life give rise to you and me

Still-life sprouts forth composing-decomposing-recomposing

Within, the darkness of the earthen womb

There is refuge from doom or gloom

Within the Temple of Bloom

Life ignites in all forms, textures and dimensions

Bursting shoots arising in awesome splendor

Eternally-emerging, diverging and converging

Unanimity a testament to the divinity of life's enduring longevity

Embarked within and beyond

The tangible consumptive senses of body, soul and mind

Silently, serenely unfolding, the creative manifestation of substance,

Form in symmetry, texture, color and design,

Off-springs rooted in the Blood of the Vine

Simply beautiful, beautifully divine

Beautifully simplistic, simplistically divine

In-Body-meant - the Temple's shrine - I am HIS - He is mine

Blooming gloriously in form - miraculously revealing the incarnation

A testivinty to the all encompassing simplistic granduer

Of the omnipresent of the Creator

A View from a Room at the Temple of Bloom

KNOWING ALL -- ALL KNOWING

Knowing now -- without question -- GOD IS omnipresent

Before the so-called beginning

Beyond the realm of the never ending

The ALPHA-OMEGA was, is, and remains a given

The light of DIVINITY resides within the recesses of our souls

The radiance of ITS light is reflective of our LOVE of GOD

Conquest -- put to rest -- overcome by GOD's loving kindness

Pontificating the present, knowing now, there is no separation

Betwixt Earth and Heaven

Stone casters living in houses of glass

Striving to be first -- How long can it last

Evangelists missing their missions

Truth-distortion an inverted condition

False messiah cometh as the son of perdition

Life-Death juxtaposition

Preaching ad nausea- without practice

Religiously pursuing the almighty dollar

Silently condoning the inquisition by our indifference

Sanctity of life - sinfully absent

Human fears cast silhouettes of Godlessness

Knowing searching for GOD is an oxymoron

The Kingdom is within and upon us

The HOLY SPIRIT is Present

In the Heart of the Soul of the True Believer

All things are now known

The harvest will be reaped according to the seeds sown

Knowing, and TRULY relating to what we have always known

We cannot live by bread alone

Science -- not GOD -- is on trial, a fact that is undeniable

Sodom-Gomorrah a now-a-day lifestyle

Deceived-deceivers existing in a state of mutual unacceptance

Undoubtedly, they can expect the unexpected

Orchestrated obsolescence -- overindulged decadence

Unquenchable thirsts of greed-self extinguishing

Now, there is no future, no past

All things being equal too nothing less

Driving -- not driven -- within a cosmic continuum

Spoken word falling on deaf ears

Searching far off when LOVE is here

Eyes to see visions impaired

Standing still -- running scared

One breath away from transcending temporality

Shedding materiality -- Overcome by spirituality

Knowing GOD is the ALPHA-OMEGA -- my Creator

Yeshua is my SAVIOR and Redeemer

The HOLY SPIRIT is my Divine Intervener

Seeds of bitterness, envy and hate

Have been exhumed from my being

All things attest to my belief -- nothing else is needed

I am by Grace a servant and believer

My inalienable rights are not contingent upon words written

By other humans – They're GOD given

My life is not my own -- I am moved soulfully by the Spirit

I have no choice but to speak the TRUTH

Regardless of its Consequences

Forgiveness, live and let live -- according to the will of Allah

By GOD's Grace alone, I will rise up from the ashes and dust

And by Divine Intervention reconcile what I must

All I know is I Trust in GOD's ALL Knowingness

Knowing All - All Knowing

GOD KNOWS

I am not here to touch the hem of your toga

Or to adjust the wreath on your ignoble head

I am not here to fight in your wars

To avenge the senseless killing of the dead

Or to live in fear of stating what needs to be said

I am not here to pursue your earthly treasures

Or to partake in your lustful pleasures

I am not here to condone sanctimonious madness

Or to remain indifferent to those who are

Commonly referred to as the ignorant masses

I am not here to partake in the demise of

A self-serving compromise

Or to foster lily-white lies

I am not here to listen obediently to never ending diatribe

Or to succumb to a dysfunctional hierarchy

I am not here to justify the unjustifiable

Or to deny the undeniable reality

Of this self-imposed inhumane condition

Nor to Sanction the Genocide, suffering and pain

Conducted in GOD's name

The living are killing to avenge the dead

From all of this suffering and inhumanity

What have we learned?

Concepts of reality promoting greed, exploitation and infidelity

GOD knows -- we have eyes to see

Those concepts border on the fringe of stark-raving insanity

I am not here to be shackled in the chains

Of your exploitive and manipulative traditions

I am not here to play your games or to bid you favor

GOD knows why I am here

To remind you there is but one Savior

To rid your temples of money changers

To expose your sinister ways

Keeping neighbor against neighbor

To expedite your extradition of pseudo empowerment

To remind you that GOD's Plan remains unchanged

And, it will be fulfilled come Judgment Day

GOD knows -- we have infinite choices -- seek His love

Or simply remain absorbed in our own vanity

GOD knows it is not my right to Judge or to be judged

Nevertheless, GOD knows,

I will go down -- standing up -- to protect my inalienable rights

I do not beg to differ with anyone, et al

GOD knows the handwriting is on the wall

GOD knows -- we have choices beyond our wildest dreams

Beyond the big bank, missing link, and/or primordial scream

GOD knows -- I pray for nothing more, nor anything less,

Than to be blessed not to partake in this shamefulness

Heavens knows GOD's love is without dimension

By GOD's grace, and our repentance, we can obtain redemption

GOD KNOWS

TRANSCENDENCE

Transcending through the corridors of creation

Destine for my ultimate destination

I am cast in the light of my present being

As a fleeting shadow on a sunlit wall

I will bear witness, reflect, than I will be no more

I do not subscribe to traditions etched in stone

As mountains have they to shall become windblown

I stand amidst the masses Yet, I journey alone

In my travels I have met many, Few, will I ever know

Civilizations founded solidly upon preconceived misconceptions

Realizations surreal - Expectations beyond realization

Intangibles immeasurably concealed

In pursuit of being consumed by the material world

Preoccupied with ritualistic diatribe -

As I witness the de-moralization of humankind

As they shred the tread of life essential for survival

In competition with the host

Predicated on those that win end up with the most

Blessed are they that are fulfilled -- buy less

May they be enriched in their transcendence

By the power of the Holy Spirit

TRANSCENDENCE

TRANSPOSURE

I am but one leaf strung in the tree of Life

In the ongoing process of transposing

Firmly planted upon the fields of

Natural understanding -- understood

The substance of my being is nurtured by self-evident truths

All things are one

From within the womb of Life I transcend

As the light of Life cast the image of my being

I seek to be all the little that I am -- a manifestation of Life

My growth and development stem beyond my roots

My branches reach beyond the limits of their tangible composition

As I embark not alone upon,

But within the never-ending-cycles of transition

From Life I draw upon the natural elements for my sustenance

Constantly seeking a balanced intake of nutrients

Not to exceed nor be less that

What is required to maintain my existence

My strength and well-being are directly related to my equanimity

The depths of my roots partially reflect

The degree of experience which I have transpired

The fruits that my tree bear are not of my own

They are attributes of my contributory involvement

Within the Natural Order

Today, I am the offspring of yesterday's dying

Tomorrow I will be the same fuel for the living

My energy form is constantly changing

Yet my Force forever remains the same

As I am, a bud taking leave --

Evolving, absorbing and revolving through

The corridors of Creation

How can one be attuned to the Order of the Universe

-- If one is not Chi's into its rhythmic verse

Whence I take leave of the tree of Life

Am I still not strung within Her web?

If these things be true -- then, let it be

-- I am Transposed

TRANSPOSURE

TRANSITION

I dwell in the now and here –

Where the sounds of silence echo above the sounds of loud noises

In a place where the illusions of darkness have

Given way to the light

Clarity is now the portrait of still-life

Within the center that maintains a balance between all extremities

'The pursuit of my understanding is now understood

All things -- together and un-together -- are one

In part what I have sought, I have found

The seemingly unending journey though

Occidental and Transcendental Thoughts

Have revealed that which always was -- and is now

That I am in part as the whole

Expanding my fundamental awareness of

The known and unknown

Actively engaged in the spiritual enhancement of

The Life Force on this Planet

Systematically contributing from within and toward the

Natural Order

My limited perspective does not distinguish between

The so-called beginning and the end

As all things are cyclical -- I transcend

TRANSITION

TAR PIT CITY

Difficult to relate -- let alone understand

Over our heads on dry land

Telecommunications systems probing deep into space

Out of touch here on Earth

Waiting on hold for tomorrow -

For what Humankind refuses to reconcile

Self-indulgences out of proportion

Captives of the laws of injustice

Friends -- Neighbors -- Perfect strangers

Jungles giving way to civilization -

As the assault against Nature rages

Biological-clock ticking --- final stages --- Humankind endangered

The mysteries of Life are many -

Those that understand them are few

Who among us can speak with experience of the here after

Great civilizations have come and vanished

As we now approach the final moment

Dinosaurs bit the dust -- as will the rest of us

The Recession's over -- the White Cliffs of Dover

Life as we know it -- is almost over

Unless, of course we chose to live in accordance with

Nature's laws

Tar Pit City

REIGNING LIGHT

See Moon and Sun

Day and night

Son's shining bright

Floating in Tsunami waves of reigning light

Juxtaposed between left and right

Reflective images of translucent light

Floating on waves of reigning light

Baptized in the twilight of enlightenment

Communing upon manna from heaven

Joyfully receiving and giving

Partaking and sharing in awe of all that which GOD is giving

Worlds without end - eternal beginnings

As our joyful hearts keep on dancing and signing

Eternal praises as we float and rise

To HE whom has risen –

Without end of beginning

We keep on dancing and singing ----

Giving thanks and praises at the oasis of Graces

Floating and flying into blissful vistas of endless horizons

Childlike and unencumbered - Growing light-years younger

We no longer thirst nor hunger

GOD's Almighty Kingdom is Reigning

Within and upon us Day and Night

REIGNING LIGHT

A Plea for Sanity

Today, I seek to beg union with people of reason

Pray tell, we will find unity

Together, once and for all let us bid farewell to life's tragedies

And well-kept sorrows

Now we shall look hunger in the face and feed it until its heart content

Let us recognize that violence will not be overcome by force

It needs to be comforted in the arms of loving kindness

Today, these things shall be done

As it is senseless to wait until tomorrow

For once let us remain silent and listen to the voice of wisdom

Let the wounded in life be healed

By love bound in forgiveness

Great needs have arisen from humanity, time and again

And in all our darkest hours Life has never failed us

Today, I stood in the presence of Beauty and gave thanks to Joy

And Prayed to GOD that Humankind respond to this

Plea for Sanity

MANY CHIEFS – MAN OF PEACE

Many Chiefs - Many Chiefs a man of Peace

Lives in a land where violence never sleeps

White man came - was Red man's guest

Then, White man put Red man to rest

On Earth - where the Sun never rises nor ever sets

Many Chiefs - Many Chiefs

Watches, but is not pleased

Witnessing the rise in civilized man's diseases

Pixie children - old and dying

Traitors - selling and buying

Black Forest's dying

The wealthy feast at the expense of the needy

Socially acceptable to be greedy

Forked- tongue's white lies

Now threaten the existence of humankind

Many Chief Speaks

Live in Peace or life as you now know it will cease

Many Chief Speaks

BLACK HANDS IN THE WHITE HOUSE

Buying in - Selling out - Greed's in -- Morales out

Rat pack's running thereabouts

Raising fears -- rising doubts

Fast foods -- slow minds - Cash flows -- hard times

Amidst a mass of brain dead mimes

Halved-baked lies -- overdone

Still life's on the run

Disinformation is no lie - Fighting wars from both sides

Weapon sales -- profits high

Indifferent to who live or dies

Long-term solution in short demand

Impending catastrophes treated with band-aid therapy

World leaders reading from the same script -

Breed fear -- get rich

Organized crime has made the switch

Terrorism's in -- Communism's out

Raising fears – rising-doubts

Buying In - Selling Out

Black Hand's in the White House

(Written and copyrighted around 2001 circa)

HELL BOUND OVERSPENT

High Tek Weapons - High Tek Weapons

That's where the BIG Bucks are spent

Neighbors' in the street - can't afford the rent

Hell Bound - Over spent

All in the interest of National Defense

Klan man cops dressed in blue - really white

Who's fooling who - let's get it right

High Tek Weps - High Tek Weps

That's where the Big Bucks are spent

To Defend what the Banks Invest

Authorities pushing traffic fines and higher taxes

The good-Earth is about to shift on its axis

Because its showdown city between the forces

High Tech Weps - High Tech Weps

That's where the BIG Bucks are spent

Hell Bound and Overspent

Sense Expansion

SIGHT

Stare into the depths of your distortion

And your visions and thoughts will become clear

SOUND

Listen beyond the sounds of loud noises

Silence is what you will hear

TOUCH

Feel and know your deepest thoughts of death

And, the meaning of life will be within your grasp

TASTE

Starve the sour bitterness of your own hate

And, the sweetness of life is what you'll taste

SMELL

Exhale the stale odors of your polluted thoughts

Breathe in the fragrant freshness of pure love

Sense Expansion

Self Acknowledgment

In order for one to know one's self in the present

One should acknowledge, understand, benefit, and

Accept one's past experiences

Identity is not confined to a specific event

It is cumulative in our journey

Life's Beauty is often just beyond the shadows of her Sorrow

We deprive ourselves today of fulfilling our dreams

Settling for tomorrow

The secrets of life are not hidden

They remain in places we have yet to visit

Journey inward and onward in pursuit of thy own complexities

Thus endeavor to be enlighten by the simplicities of life's mysteries

Exposure to life and the natural forces

Are often thought of by humanity

As unnecessary hardships

Civilizations have risen and come to past

Still humankind sees itself apart from Nature

The Wisdom of Life is not obtained in a state of alienation

Her Wisdom is bountiful and self fulfilling for those that participate

How can we acknowledge the gift of sustenance?

If, all we have ever done is to stuff ourselves

Can we understand the plight of our fellow human-beings'

Who, struggle with hunger, sickness, and poverty, as a way of life

Can we ever hope to find enlightenment,

If we choose to remain in darkness?

Should we forever deny ourselves elation,

Because we shun exposure?

How can we ever come to know and love Life?

If, we do not pursue and acknowledge our misunderstandings

To pontificate our differences

Each of us should acknowledge that

Birth is the gateway to life everlasting;

For I Am One - and we are many - Life in the form of Humanity

SELF ACKNOWLEDGMENT

INSIGHT ON MY OUTLOOK

From within my visions reflect beyond

Upon fertile pastures where the land an people are one

This relationship is a reflection of mutual respect

Wherein, all things come from the Earth

I lived within Life's cycles even before I was given birth

As I am composed of the elements - fire, air water and earth

Within the never ending cycles I too transcend

From one state to another - Now I am Human

Embarked upon an endeavor to plow and uproot

The fields of destruction, deceit and desolation

Pursuing all would be obstacles without hesitation

Weeding the soils of distortion, corruption and confusion

Planting in their place the seeds of Truth

Nourished by the Wisdom of the ages

The fruits of my labor will withstand the drift of fugitive contaminants

As my strength is furnished from roots deeply planted,

Which, have been weathered by the natural forces

Founded upon the fact that I am

A part of the all giving Life-Force on this Planet

And to live accordingly

Insight on My Outlook

Now Here Always Was

All that was meant to mean something means nothing now

That which was -- is not

That which was not -- now is

All that which seemed involved has been made simple

The light I had seen then was naked darkness

The darkness I see now is pure light

All that I thought I knew - I know not of anymore

I am younger and ignorant than the day before

Now I hear the birds calling from the trees -

Singing life is to be lived freely

With the echo of the wind reflecting identity in a silent breeze

The trees are growing taller restoring their leaves

The grass is now the cushion of my bed

The rhythms of the earth are the heart beat within my head

Where there are no longer thoughts of death

For I am now standing on Life's steps

Becoming more aware with each and every breath

I have awakened in the land where the sun no longer sets

Where Beauty is as Beauty's met, wherein

The essence of Love is well-kept

Now Here --- Nowhere

JOYFUL BEING – BEING JOYFUL

I witness JOY in all her splendor

Transcending age --- overcoming gender

Divinely sharing this blessing with humanity

A moment of peace --- a lasting glimpse of sanity

Outwardly striking accord with the inner core of other souls

Consoling --- being consoled

Knowing --- being known

Moving through life relatively unscathed

Joyfully reaching out embracing loneliness and despair

With a few heartfelt words and a loving gaze

Joy-riding high --- raising our spirits

As we gave thanks and praise to GOD for having been graced

By the presence of this JOYFUL being -- being Joyful

JOYFUL BEING --- BEING JOYFUL

SPIRITUAL BLISSFULNESS

I am the spirit shrouded in the flesh

My soulful existence is death-defying

I am a humanifestation of Life that reigns - Eternally

The contents of my intangible being is neither contained by,

Nor, limited to, what is commonly conceived as all knowing

Beyond it, exist the realm of the unknown - knowingness

Where the spirit of my being transcends the void of nothingness

Beyond the abyss of nothing less than absolute blissfulness

I am --- You are

The SPIRITUAL Manifestation of GOD

By the Grace of our Lord Jesus Christ

Empowered by the Holy Spirit

To carry out GOD's Will

All the days of this life

SPIRITUAL BLISS

I AM - AM I

It is only I - A lowly servant of the Most High

I cannot stumble or follow in the footsteps of other humans

If, by Grace, I am raised up and led by the Hand of GOD

How am I to find fault in my sisters and brothers

If it is not to be found within my heart

For the Love of GOD - I cannot hate

Eyes to See - I live by blind Faith

Lord knows, Forgiveness is a given

It is never too late

Putting the desires of the flesh to Death

Enables the Soul to Resurrect

In pursuit of Salvation - Indifferent to survival

Immersing my Soul - In a Spiritual Revival

Seeking the Divine Light of the SON

To be empowered by the ALMIGHTY ONE

Knowing - no longer anticipating - Alleluia – Kingdom's come

Expectations beyond realization

Divinely sensing this GOD sent Revelation

I AM - AM I

Passing On Over to the Great Beyond

Passing on over to the other side

Is an ongoing continuum on a cosmic-ride

God knows our souls never die they just move on to the by, and by

If the truth be known with GOD in our lives we are never alone

Life is more than pure coincidence

When you sum it all up its simply divine intervention

Shut down your mind - open yourself to your soul

Embrace the Truth and let everything else go

Always remember GOD is in control

Fear does not have to be feared;

It is only when we choose it to be so

The Word of GOD is without question

HE has provided us with a way out through His Son - YESHUA

The Chosen - Begotten - One

Do not lose Faith

Never, is to Late - Knock and He Shall answer

We All can Live Now and forevermore in the Hereafter

Just a few words in Passing

Passing on to the Great Beyond

God Is

Omnipresent

Hence, not absent

Accordingly,

The unaccountability

Absence of God's

Presence

Is our not being accountable or present

In the Omnipresence of

GOD

UNIVERSAL FIELD & TRACK MEET – CHAMPIONS OF DEFEATS

Contestants to compete are West Lead Head -- Occidental Man –

The outside-record-maker – versus -

East Lead Feet -- Transcendental Man -- the inside-record maker

At the starting line we have none other than Father Time

It seems as though we have a record-breaking crowd on hand

As the fans conduct themselves in the usual manner of

Loud noises of boos and cheers

Oh! There's the Good Humor man – shouting, I scream,

I scream individual flavors from the variety cycle

Today's special, cherry the vanilla

And be yourself and the hell with it

With no artificial sweeteners to cause cancer

I screamed, I screamed, but no one answered

Now as the contestants get in to a steadfast position

At the starting line

The crowd grows silent in body and mind

Anticipating the sound of the blank gun

As the sounds of silence grew

Their indifference vanished

And smiles were replenished upon their faces

As the sounds of silence became simply greater

The outcome of the race

Which they had lost interests in

Ended when it started

By each failing to recognize the need for the other

Reflecting the image of man which falls short of incomplete

Being known as the Champions of Defeat

West Lead Head and East Lead Feet

UNIVERSAL FIELD AND TRACK MEET

Seeds of Distinction

As is - I Am - Firmly Planted upon the

Fields of Natural Understanding

Embedded deep beneath the surface,

Where the essences of my being is made whole

Receiving nourishment through the All Giving Source

As the seed of Life takes form - I Am - only that which you are

One seed - seeking to absorb

Receiving nourishment from within my roots

Stemming beneath as above

Bearing the fruits of distinguished individuality

Each as All - All As ONE

Together receiving that which has been given,

Which is only as whence it began

By the Sharing of that which, has been given

Thus the cycle of Life is now - as ever

Sustained in Balance with Itself

Thus I Am - Only, that which you are

The total effect of the planting - growing and harvest

As one crop - reaping the Truth

In body a seed - in mind the Fruit

Thus the sharing of that which has been received -

And given - from whence

The seed of Love was - as is - embedded deep

Within the pastures of natural

Understanding – understood

Nourished through the source of our being - as ONE seed

Rooted beneath as above - As all seeds as one Love

Thus I Am - only that which you are

In part - as ONE - the Living Spirit

United together as one GOD

SEEDS OF DISTINCTION

CREATION

By the Light Within

As the all As ONE

Sea - Man – Sun

See Man's Son

As the Making is of one - Love

I am - You are

Let IT Be

Man's Son Seen

Enlightening The Absolute image within our present Being

GOD

As is - I Am - A Man - Amen

CREATION

Oh! God

There is so little that I know

So much I need to understand

For decades I have observed the seasons come and go

I have experienced the pure fragrance of Spring

And the warmth of the Summer sun

I witnessed the beauty of the Autumn Sky

And the chill of the Winter snows

Each experience is more breath taking than the last

As only now I begin to grasp Nature's simplistic grandeur

I gaze upon the sunlit waters

As the birds sing their ancestral songs beneath the autumn sky

I breathe the Breath of Life

My mind reflects and answers, is there a need to question why?

Oh! GOD

EXISTENCE AS IS

I Am - only a minute particle

In essence a mere grain of sand

Yet the all of my entirety is brought forth

At which point the sea retreats

As its tide withdraws

The mystery of my origin silently unfolds

Revealing my presence from whence it always was

And, is now

Upon the shore of what shall be known as the living substance

Thus in part - I Am, only that which you are

In truth - all of that which was - now is -

And shall be - after and forever more

Momentarily seeking to absorb the nourishment

That will reveal the source of my ignorance

From within darkness

As the sun "rises" and takes form

So be it as the breaking of the dawn

Giving birth to the seeds of empirical self-knowledge

Enabling me to be all of the little which I Am

I Am, only that which you are

Existing as is

In a brief instance

Seeking to reveal the nature of my being

The element of identity

As a particle of sand

One sure mind - I Am

Thus HE is within my soul

As I Am now

The Spirit of the Son in the likeness of man

Now as the approaching tide returns

Washing my being from upon the shore

Albeit, I shall forever remain

In part - as the whole

I acknowledge my so-called limitedness which reveals my all

I envision the portrait of still-life reflecting from within

Beauty, Harmony, Truth, Understanding-Understood

As the ALL - Absolute

As one Sea-Man-Son

As the making is made of ONE

Through the Creator, Almighty, and ALL Loving

Thus I Am, only that which you are

ALL as ONE

For sure

The Spirit of the Living GOD

EXISTENCE AS IS

ETERNAL ORDER

The natural forces are fixed and yet ever-changing

The Life Force lives -- giving life through death

As it has, is now, and will continue in perpetuity of itself

My life, itself is not everlasting - yet life is

Within the intricate web of life for this eternal instance

The Spirit of Life dwells within my being

As I seek to overcome my limitedness, knowing I am, in part,

All things, and to live accordingly

Cyclically the mysteries of life silently unfold,

Revealing all things, yet nothing new

In my brief instance, I live, share and forgive

At one point, my past, present and future will be one in the same

Thenceforth, I will not fall prey to the illusions

Of what I should have been

Rather, I will gratefully accept myself for whom and what I represent

A living manifestation of Life in the form of Man

My existence passes like a fleeting shadow on a sunlit wall

It is, then, it is no more

Living as always, in accordance with the Eternal Order

ETERNAL ORDER

BABBLE-ON BABYLONIANS

Diatribists' flapping their lips

So-called leaders reading from the dooms-day script

New World Order a one-way ticket on a sinking ship

World leaders reading from the same old-script

Breed fear -- Get rich quick

Timeless Messages - Endless passages

As the distance between the masses enhances

Right-wing revolution cashing in

On abortion, welfare, Satan and sin

As the liberal contingent espouses equality for all

From the perches of their out-of-touch Park Avenue Palaces

Mortgaging off the future to pay off past debts

As we continue to cut a hole in the Earth's safety-net

Shredding the web of life at a break-neck pace

Assuring the mutual destruction of the human race

As politicians, big business and scientists

Speak out of both sides of their Orifices

Low lifer status has been elevated to a higher place

For the right price you can live in disgrace

Prisons are warehouses that profit the rich

Who penalize the poor but exempt themselves

Children pay the highest price for world debt

Their future is now a thing of the past

Organized disorder promoted by the New World Order

History of civilizations a cavalcade of cultures vanished

Who lost touch with the Natural Order

As we now await our turn to choose a new path of perish

BABBLE-ON

EPILOGUE

Truth-De-Code-It's **Empowerment:** We are blessed and endowed with inalienable rights, and it is our responsibility to become empowered and exercise those rights accordingly.

"We the People", as individuals, consumers, and citizens have and will cast our votes by the choices we make every day, what we buy, from whom, and where we trade, taking steps to ensure that are actions are sustainable, viable, minimizing our adverse impacts on others and the life-support system. It is imperative to be responsible for our actions, for our sake, and for the benefit of others in pursuit of truth, liberty, peace, security, freedom and happiness.

As we learn there is so much more to life than we can begin to imagine, let alone articulate. Albeit, let us not limit our imagination or expectations; life for each of us is a one-of-a-kind journey.

Life in all its glory, wonder and splendor, as we all have come to know in on our journey, is rife with challenges, mystery, uncertainties and awe-inspiring creativity. As is for each of us, and all- living beings, Earth, water and space, are common bonds we all share; tethered to this life-sustaining terrestrial and oceanic sphere. As a people, we should learn to revere and not fear life's bewildering, challenging, and unpredictable experiences; to treat all life as sacred.

For many of us, Life's simplicity is, at times, shrouded by its breathtaking and overwhelming immensity. Its secrets and wisdom are subtly revealed to all those that enable themselves to establish a meaningful and sustainable relationship with and in life.

An enthusiastic passionate open-mindedness often unlocks life's mysteries, many of which allude and perplex the best of minds, since laying the foundation of civilizations and "fixing" the hands of time. In the interlude of this enigma, we have the innate ability to be transfigured-in-perpetuity.

Eschatological prophecy attests to the fulfillment of Parousia, Second Coming, in the midst, as written, all things are to be reconciled in accordance with the Divine Plan. Evil is on the way to burning itself out, raising fears, rising doubts, will be overcome by Truth, change and self-empowerment.

Adapting to a way-of-life that ensures humankind's health, safety and sustainability, while empowering ourselves to actively-cultivate a reverent relationship with Nature. For our sake, it is imperative that we acknowledge and develop a richer and clearer understanding of our dependence upon this Earth's fragile, yet dynamic and creative life-support system. Implementing such actions will empower us to improve our interactive-relationships with all-things and help to make our home on this planet a more harmonious and safer place to live.

Life is a limitless-cosmic continuum, once we get over the "this is it" – Death -preconceived misconceptions, embedded deception, and/or the intentionally misleading concepts we-the-people have unwillingly or unknowingly subscribed to as a way-of-life, which is now threatening our existence, and life itself; and, that is the Truth.

In truth, we are all sustained by and through the endless bounty provided by Mother Nature. Our interactive and life-death-defying experience in-the-making, is, in and by itself, a testament to our immortality.

Empirically, wisdom gained through life's trials and tribulations enables us to discern the experience, within and from a multidimensional perspective - infinitum; empowering us to live our lives' accordingly. The concept of living in the flesh inspires a mind of be-wonderment, as we rise up upon this earthen crust.

Intangible thoughts manifested in the cortex of our being, as we brainstorm in the cerebral hemispheres; materializing our imagination and realizations, as our inquiring nature provokes chemical-electrical brain synapses; pontificating the cerebral-gaps betwixt ethereal concepts to thought realizations.

In life, we are literally metamorphosing from substance to Spirit. In this life-giving experience, we simultaneously interact upon a myriad of current and age-old thought provoking issues, exponentially. Now, however, necessity requires unanimity.

To My Fellow Human Beings: May the blessings of the Creator's Great Spirit of Peace, Love and charitable Forgiveness dwell within your being - may your visions become a reality, and your reality a humanifestation of your dreams.

In the Words of Yeshua-Christos: "Love your neighbors as I have Loved You".

In so doing, God will be well pleased - Porgans.

Circa 2013 A.D. Parousia-Paschal (Gregorian calendar).

Although, all rights are reserved, written permission to reprint will be granted as requested. Peace, Grace, and Prosperity be with you in all ways; always.

ABOUT THE AUTHOR:
A REBEL BORN FOR A JUST CAUSE

The author is a self-raised, empirically educated, and as an entrepreneur created a way of life to pursue his passion and to sustain his life's work. Thanks, be to the One God.

Since childhood, he has been endowed with a seemingly unquenchable thirst for Truth, wisdom, and spiritual fulfillment. Porgans lives in the present, a gift for which he is eternally grateful. He has come to know, believe, and recognize that by the Creator's Grace: All things are possible; life itself is a testament to that fact, regardless if one is a believer. Truth avails itself to all who seek, and living in the Truth can set us free from anyone or anything, hence true enlightenment.

Life's experiences teach us that seeking Truth can be viewed as a double-bladed sword. In the course of life Porgans always, and in every way, exercises independence as an individual, questioning authority, and relentlessly resisting all forms of oppression, deception and their irreconcilable consequences; even in the face of overwhelming opposition.

Much of his life has been expended observing the ways of nature and those of man, adapting to Nature's law. Along the journey, he has studied a myriad of issues that have perplexed and altered the existence of civilizations since their inceptions; many such issues are prevalent today on a global scale.

In the process, he has identified, designed, and implemented cost-effective and practical solutions that have and continue to empower change; minimizing, deterring or eliminating large-scale adversities in regions located in North America's West; from the Front Range in the Rocky Mountains to the Pacific Ocean, extending to the Canadian and Mexican borders. Areas impacted by natural- and/or human-induced conditions, finding adaptive and sustainable solutions to minimize individual, government, and commerce impacts on the life-support system, which makes our lives possible.

Truth De-Code-It reflects upon the formula that the wealthy-pluto-crats use to amass and maintain ill-gained fortunes, by exploiting the public's tax-base, credit rating, natural resources, and politi-cally-held offices.

Out of necessity he has shed light on specific conditions asso-ciated with the Era of Deception, clarifying half-truths, rectifying political corruption, deterring selective-regulatory enforcement tactics adversely impacting the economy, families, and critical natural resources and placing national, state and regions at higher risks, while creating additional "stressors" upon a reportedly over-burden life-support system.

During the past several decades, the author has identified and implemented measures to ensure accurate accountability of government's management and track-record in performing its ob-ligation to protect the public and its trust resources.

By Grace, he continues to intervene as a Solutionist, and wit-ness, to identify all factors and forces (real or orchestrated) on a plethora of issues; conditions contributing to socioeconomic and environmental instability, which undermine the economy and our quality of life.

The author's decades of experience have--and continue to be--focused on the development of viable, cost-effective solutions to remedy government-corporate-induced crises; and to bring ourselves to a state of homeostasis. These solutions also aim to negate further adverse impacts which would have otherwise posed a significant financial debt to the taxpayers and irrevocable adverse ecological hazards to humankind, other species, and the environment.

As a servant of God, fellow-human-being, kindred-spirit, and, as a de-facto public trustee, he shares these thoughts with Thee. FYI: www.plantarysolutionaries.org.

CPSIA information can be obtained
at www.ICGtesting.com
Printed in the USA
LVHW022107190423
744849LV00009B/35

9 781432 794859